JULIET SEAR

Kawaii Cakes

PHOTOGRAPHY BY
JACQUI MELVILLE

JULIET SEAR

Kawaii Cakes

**ADORABLE & CUTE
JAPANESE-INSPIRED
CAKES & TREATS**

hardie grant books

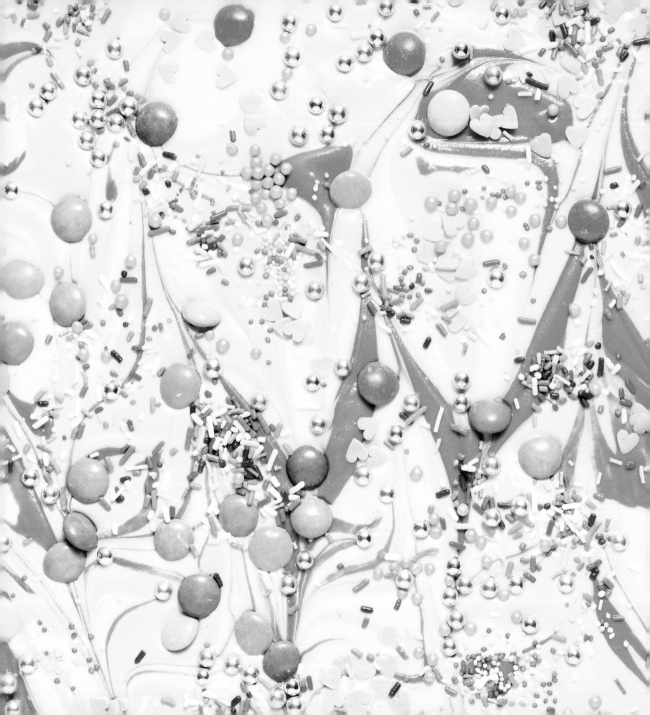

Contents
内容

Introduction

Welcome to *Kawaii Cakes*!

What does kawaii mean? Some people don't know or haven't heard of it... YET. But all those kawaii fans out there know very well – it is a Japanese word and it means cute, lovable and adorable. It's widely used in Japanese pop culture, particularly among anime and manga fans, and has been around for decades. You can see it in fashions where the clothing is an array of bright and pastel colours, often with lots of accessories including plush toys and cute icons and emoticons, such as hearts, stars, bows and rainbows.

If it is cute, lovable and adorable, it's kawaii :)

The kawaii trend is growing across the world, and there are many recognisable kawaii characters, from Sanrio's world-famous Hello Kitty to Miffy and Friends, and the Pokémon phenomenon. These are just the tip of the iceberg when you consider the overwhelming number of items out there with kawaii themes.

Pinterest and Instagram are awash with kawaii designs in many different forms. You can see more kawaii in high-street stores, where regular items are made super-cute by adding big eyes and cartoonish faces, giving them a childlike, innocent look. And it's not just bento, sushi, and all kinds of savoury food – people are bringing kawaii to life through cakes, baking and pastry treats. What could be sweeter?

OVEN TEMPERATURES: these are given for fan ovens. If you are using a conventional oven, increase the heat by around 20°C (50°F). For best results, use an oven thermometer.

Baking and kawaii make a perfect pairing and go together like best friends.

I LOVE making edible art and, of course, baking is my passion, so I was inspired to write this book full of cute baked characters in lovable styles, to bring a touch of kawaii to my cakes, biscuits and treats. All these recipes are super-easy – I hope you'll enjoy them, and have great fun sharing them with friends and family. Many are perfect for celebrations and also for edible gifts. The first section of the book focuses on the adorable kawaii designs and will give you lots of inspirational ideas, followed by recipes for the bakes, fillings, frostings and icings. The book is easy to use and I'm sure, once you've experimented with pastel colours, rainbows, clouds and kawaii expressions using edible pens, icings and chocolate, you'll be creating your own kawaii designs too.

This book is full of colourful cute treats with personalities – from rainbow sprinkle Piñata Cloud Cookies (page 10) to a Sweet Unicorn Cake (page 29). I also love the kawaii Christmas characters on pages 27, 42 and 46 – in fact, it's hard to choose my favourite! Once you've mastered the basic techniques and recipes, you'll soon be able to craft your own kawaii characters.

I hope you enjoy making these delicious treats and that they bring a hint of magic to your baking that will delight everyone who eats them.

Please share pictures of your bakes using the hashtag #kawaiicakes

Kawaii Bakes

かわいい焼く

Unicorn Poop 💩 Iced Gem Cookies

These are SO cute and make perfect party treats or gifts. They look lovely in a bag tied with rainbow ribbon. I used a fluted cutter to make round, crinkled cookies but you can use any type of cutter.
Makes 24

01 To make the rainbow poop topping, fill the 4 piping bags (without nozzles) with each colour of icing.

02 Fit the large piping bag with the star nozzle. Snip the end of each small bag so that you have a 1 cm (½ in) hole and carefully place each bag in the larger bag so that the tips reach evenly into the star nozzle. It helps to put a clip at the end of the large bag to stop the icing from spilling out of the top.

03 Squeeze the icing onto the cookies by holding the bag in a vertical position, and moving in circles around each cookie, starting from the outside edge, winding inwards and building height to create a peak.

04 Leave to dry overnight. To speed up the drying process you can place the cookies in a low oven at about 70°C (140°F/Gas low) for 30 minutes, then turn off the heat and leave for 2 hours.

Piñata Cloud Cookies

These cute clouds have fun rainbow sprinkles inside for a sweet surprise. Instead of using pink dusting powder for the cheeks you could use edible pink pen, and smudge it. *Makes 10*

STUFF YOU'LL NEED

- 1 batch Vanilla Sugar Cookie dough (page 70)
- plain (all-purpose) flour, for dusting
- cloud cutter or template (page 95), plus round cutter (smaller than the cloud cutter)
- a little soft-peak white Royal Icing (page 89), in a piping bag fitted with a number 2 round nozzle, for sticking
- 150 g (5 oz) white sugar paste (fondant)
- sprinkles of your choice
- pink edible dusting powder, for cheeks
- a little soft-peak black Royal Icing (page 89), in a piping bag fitted with a number 1.5 round nozzle, for face details

SKILL LEVEL MODERATE

01 Preheat the oven to 180°C (350°F/Gas 4). Dust your work surface lightly with flour. Roll the cookie dough out to a thickness of about 4 mm (¼ in).

02 Using the cutter or template, cut out 3 clouds per cookie (around 30 clouds in total).

Method continues on the next page...

03 Line a baking tray with baking parchment and place the cloud-shaped cookies on top, leaving a 2.5 cm (1 in) gap between them. Cut a small circle inside 10 of the clouds to give space for the sprinkles. These clouds will form the middle cookie layer. Place the cookies in the oven and bake for 10–12 minutes.

04 Roughly pipe a little white royal icing over 10 of the plain cookies (without a hole).

05 Roll out the white sugar paste to a thickness of about 2 mm (⅛ in) and cut out 10 cloud shapes, one for the top of each iced cookie.

09 Pour in the sprinkles to fill the cavity, then pipe more royal icing around the edge of the middle cut-out cookie.

10 Top with a sugar paste cookie and press down lightly. Repeat with the other cookies and leave to dry for a few hours.

06 Place the sugar paste clouds on top of the iced cookies.

07 To assemble the cookies, roughly pipe a little royal icing around the edges of the holes in the 10 cut-out cookies.

08 Press the cut-out cookies, iced side down, on top of the remaining plain cookies, to create the middle and bottom cookie layer.

11 When dry enough, you can add cute faces to your piñata clouds using pink dusting powder and black royal icing or edible pen (page 87).

TOP TIP:
See how to add faces to your bakes on page 87.

Avocados

STUFF YOU'LL NEED

- 1 batch ready-baked Vanilla Sugar Cookies (page 70), shaped with cutters or using the template on page 95
- icing (confectioners') sugar, for dusting
- 500 g (1 lb 2 oz) white sugar paste (fondant), coloured cream with a drop of yellow food colouring
- a little soft-peak white Royal Icing (page 89), in a piping bag fitted with a number 2 round nozzle, for sticking
- green, brown and pink edible dusting powders
- a little vodka or gin
- tortilla chips (optional)
- black edible food pen (fine-tip), for face details

SKILL LEVEL EASY

Avocados are one of my favourite foods and they are super-cute as kawaii cookies. These are made in a similar way to the Piñata Cloud Cookies (page 10). You can use the avocado template on page 95. I actually used a cutter shaped like an Easter egg! *Makes 16–20*

01 Dust your work surface with icing sugar, then roll out the white sugar paste. Cut avocado shapes out of the paste using the template.

02 Roughly pipe a little royal icing around the edges of each cookie. Stick the sugar paste avocado shapes onto the cookies and leave to dry for a few hours, or ideally overnight.

03 Using a plate as a paint palette, sprinkle separate piles of the green, brown and pink dusting powders and mix each colour with a little vodka or gin to make a paint. Use a small brush to paint the green edge, the brown stone and the pink cheeks. Decorate your cookies with faces using edible pen (page 87). You can also decorate little tortilla chip companions for your avocados!

Lambykins Cookies

I was inspired to make these by some super cute puffy stickers I found — I just knew they would work as iced sugar cookies. They are so kawaii and perfect for a springtime treat! *Makes 12*

01 Before decorating these sweet cookies, dust your work surface with a little icing sugar and roll out the peach-coloured sugar paste very thinly. Using a round cookie cutter or the template, cut out the faces for the lambs.

Method continues on the next page...

STUFF YOU'LL NEED

- 1 batch ready-baked sugar cookies in any flavour (I used a mix of vanilla and chocolate flavours, page 70), shaped using cutters or the template on page 96
- icing (confectioners') sugar, for dusting
- 60 g (2 oz) pale peach-coloured sugar paste (fondant)
- 4 cm (1½ in) round cookie cutter or lamb face template (page 96)
- a little soft-peak white Royal Icing (page 89), in a piping bag fitted with a number 2 round nozzle, for sticking
- a little soft-peak Royal Icing (page 89) in pastel shades of your choice, in piping bags fitted with round number 2 nozzles, for outline
- a little runny Royal Icing (page 89), in the same pastel shades as the soft-peak icing, in piping bags (about 150 g/5 oz per colour), for flooding
- black edible food pen (fine-tip), for face details

SKILL LEVEL MODERATE

03　Carefully pipe a wavy outline of pastel soft-peak icing neatly around the edges of the cookies and around the faces.

Cute!

02　Pipe some white soft-peak royal icing onto each cookie and stick on the sugar paste cut-outs. Smooth over with your hands.

04 Flood each cookie with the matching coloured runny icing, leaving the face clear. Allow to dry for a few hours, ideally overnight.

05 Once dry, add sweet kawaii facial expressions with edible black pen to bring them to life (page 87). Adorable!

Kitty Cookies

These look adorable in caramels, chocolates and powder grey, or even in pastel colours for super-cute versions. As well as white royal icing, I used food colouring gels in black, caramel and baby pink. *Makes 20–24*

01. Pipe soft-peak royal icing around the edges of the cookie shapes in your different colours.

02. Flood the centre of the kitty face in a runny royal icing in matching colours. You can make them two- or three-tone – just have fun! Leave to dry for a few hours or ideally overnight.

03. Using the black edible pen add the nose and mouth, then some tiny whiskers to make them look puuurrr-fect (page 87). Add dots of runny white royal icing to create the shimmer on the eyes. Use pink dusting powder to add sweet cheeks. You can add a little runny pink royal icing for the insides of the ears.

STUFF YOU'LL NEED

- 1 batch ready-baked Vanilla Sugar Cookies (page 70), shaped with cutters or the templates on page 91
- soft-peak Royal Icing (page 89) in your chosen colours, in piping bags fitted with number 2 round piping nozzles, for outline
- runny Royal Icing, in the same shades as the soft-peak icing (about 150 g/5 oz per colour), in piping bags, for flooding
- black edible food pens (fine-tip), for face details
- pink edible dusting powder, for cheeks

SKILL LEVEL
MODERATE

Best Friends

SKILL LEVEL
MODERATE

There's nothing cuter than pairs of perfectly matched characters, like these Milk & Cookies buddies. I particularly love the Strawberries & Cream ones with the Peanut Butter & Jelly Toast pals. It's such fun – you can really be creative and make any templates you like. *Makes 20*

01   For the milk bottle cookies, pipe soft-peak baby-blue icing around the edge of your cookies. Next, pipe a smaller bottle shape in the middle using white soft-peak royal icing. Flood the outer area with the runny blue icing, and the middle with the runny white icing.

02   For the cookie buddies, pipe soft-peak caramel icing around the edges of the cookie shapes, then flood with the caramel runny icing. Finish with drops of runny brown icing for the chocolate chips.

03   For the Strawberries & Cream and Peanut Butter & Jelly Toast cookies, follow the same method for the Milk & Cookies but use the appropriate icing colours. Remember to pipe the outline of each section first, before flooding each one alternately.

04   Leave the iced cookies for a few hours or overnight to dry.

05   For their adorable faces, pipe black dots for eyes, then pipe a small white dot for the shine using the white soft-peak icing. Add a cheeky smile with black edible pen, and use pink edible dusting powder for their cute, tiny cheeks (page 87).

Halloween Chocolate Cookies

These cute Halloween cookies are not spooky, just kooky! They are super-fun versions of Halloween icons we know and love. *Makes 20–24*

01 For the skulls, bats and sweetie cookies, pipe the outlines with the soft-peak icing, then flood with the matching runny icing. Pipe the extra details on top, once the icing is dried.

02 For the pumpkin cookies, pipe the outline of each section first, before flooding each one alternately, leaving about 20 minutes to dry in between. Draw on the face details with black edible pen and finish with pink dusting powder for the cheeks (page 87).

TOP TIP:
See templates on page 94–95 for Halloween cookie shapes.

Gingerbread Christmas Decorations

Have yourself a kawaii Christmas! These decorations are so yummy and look amazing hanging on the tree. I've used a spicy gingerbread biscuit. For the alternative shapes, see page 74. *Makes 16–20*

01 Decorate the cookies by outlining with soft-peak icing and flooding the shapes with the matching runny icing. For the candy canes, pipe diagonal stripes and flood alternately with pink and white.

02 Allow to dry for several hours, ideally overnight, then add the face detail with soft-peak icing and edible pens.

03 If you wish to add little shimmers of light to the adorabaubles and stars, you can drop some white runny icing over the block colour in the top corner while the icing is wet.

04 For the trees, pipe on extra details in soft-peak royal icing. For the gingerbread men, pipe on outfit details and draw faces using edible pens and dusting powder.

05 Allow to set until dry, then place or hang on the tree with coloured string, or wrap in little cellophane bags to give as gifts.

TOP TIP:
Remove the biscuits from the oven after 8 minutes and create holes by plunging a straw into the dough. Return the biscuits to the oven to finish cooking. Use twine to hang the decorations from the tree.

STUFF YOU'LL NEED

- 1 pre-layered cake (page 78)
- icing (confectioners') sugar, for dusting
- 1.25 kg (2 lb 12 oz) white sugar paste (fondant)
- 30 cm (12 in) gold cake drum, for display
- cake smoothers
- 66 cm (26 in) white ribbon
- a little soft-peak white Royal Icing (page 89), in a piping bag fitted with a number 2 round nozzle, for sticking
- 40 g (1½ oz) black sugar paste (fondant)
- 5 cm (2 in) round cutter
- 60 g (2 oz) pastel pink sugar paste (fondant)
- unicorn nose template on page 97
- black edible food pen (fine-tip), for face details
- 250 g (9 oz) pastel yellow sugar paste (fondant)
- ice-cream cone, for horn
- edible gold shimmer spray and gold glitter
- 1 larger piping bag, fitted with large open star nozzle (1M)
- 500 g (1 lb 2 oz) Basic Vanilla Bean Buttercream (page 86) in four pastel colours, in piping bags
- cocktail sticks
- gold brush pen

**SKILL LEVEL
DIFFICULT**

Sweet 🦄 Unicorn Cake

I used four layers of the Fluffy Vanilla Cake (page 72) for this cake, making it nice and tall – it looks really effective. I also coloured the layers, so there's lots of rainbow fun inside the cake as well as on the outside – it looks really sweet and goes well with the rainbow mane. *Makes 1 cake*

01 First, fill and coat the cake according to the instructions on pages 78–79, then leave to firm up and set in the fridge for 1 hour.

02 Dust your work surface with icing sugar and roll out the white sugar paste to a circle large enough to cover the top and sides of the cake – about 50 cm (20 in).

03 Pick up the sheet of icing using the pin, lift up and drape over the cake.

Method continues on the next page...

04 Smooth it down with your hands, encouraging the icing to stick to the sides. Lift it up if it starts to fold. You can place any creases to the back or side and cover with the piped mane.

05 Once the icing is smoothed all over the cake, trim around the base with a sharp knife. Keep the off-cuts to make the ears.

06 Place the cake onto the gold cake drum. Using cake smoothers with firm pressure, polish the top and the sides.

07 Wrap the white ribbon around the bottom of the cake, sticking the ends together with royal icing. Make sure the join is at the back. Leave the cake overnight, before adding the other details.

12 To make the horn, take about 200 g (7 oz) of the yellow sugar paste, roll into a long sausage and flatten it a little with your palm.

13 Stick a small blob of the sugar paste on the bottom of the cone to make a secure base, then pipe a little soft-peak royal icing over the ice-cream cone to make it sticky.

14 Now wind the fondant sausage around the cone, from the base to the tip, making a point at the top. Reserve any excess sugar paste for the ears.

15 Spray with gold shimmer spray and sprinkle with a little gold glitter. Stick on the top of the cake using royal icing to secure.

08 To make the large round eyes, thinly roll out the black sugar paste and cut out circles with the 5 cm (2 in) round cutters.

09 To make the pink nose, roll out the pink sugar paste and cut around the template.

10 Use the white royal icing to stick the nose and eyes onto the front of the cake.

11 Flatten balls of white sugar paste to make white circles for the shine on the eyes. Secure with royal icing. With black edible pen, make an eyelash flick on each eye, and add the nose and mouth detail.

16 Fill the piping bags with the coloured buttercream, following the technique for the Unicorn Poop Iced Gem Cookies (page 9, step 2).

17 Pipe the mane over the cake in small circles, starting from the middle, in front of the horn, then swirling out.

18 To finish, make the ears. Take the remaining white sugar paste and split in two. Roll into balls, then to a cone, then flatten out slightly.

Do the same with the remaining yellow sugar paste, and stick this to the front of each white ear. Stand the ears behind the piped buttercream mane and prop them up with cocktail sticks (you can remove these later). Paint over the yellow with gold brush pen. Alternatively, you can use pink sugar paste for the ears to match the face.

Rainbow Swirl Cupcakes

So pretty and colourful, these cupcakes will delight your friends and family. They're as delicious to the eye as they are to the taste buds! For added fun you can split your cake recipe into four batches and colour each quarter of the mixture a different colour, then pipe little layers of cake batter into the cupcake tin for a double rainbow effect. *Makes 12*

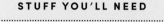

STUFF YOU'LL NEED

- 12 ready-baked cupcakes (Fluffy Vanilla Cake, page 72)
- large piping bag
- food colouring gels (I used purple, yellow, green, blue and pink)
- large open star nozzle (1M)
- 600 g (1 lb 5 oz) Basic Vanilla Bean Buttercream (page 86)
- bag clip

SKILL LEVEL EASY

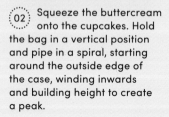

01 Turn the piping bag inside out, then drizzle with strips of the gel colours to create stripes. Turn the bag right side out, then fit it with the star nozzle and fill with buttercream. Clip the bag to keep it all in.

02 Squeeze the buttercream onto the cupcakes. Hold the bag in a vertical position and pipe in a spiral, starting around the outside edge of the case, winding inwards and building height to create a peak.

03 The colour will be blended onto the buttercream, giving a lovely rainbow swirl effect.

Kawaii Sweetheart Cupcakes ♡

Cheeky love hearts with kawaii expressions top these velvety chocolate cupcakes. They make a lovely treat for Valentine's Day. *Makes 14*

STUFF YOU'LL NEED

- **14 ready-baked Chocolate Cupcakes (page 75)**
- **750 g (1 lb 10 oz) Belgian Chocolate Ganache Buttercream (page 87), in a piping bag fitted with a large open star nozzle (1M)**
- **icing (confectioners') sugar for dusting**
- **150 g (5 oz) red sugar paste (fondant)**
- **5 cm (2 in) heart-shaped cutter**
- **soft-peak white and black Royal Icing (page 89), in piping bags fitted with number 1.5 round nozzles, for face details**

SKILL LEVEL EASY

01. Pipe the chocolate buttercream over the cupcakes, following the technique on page 32, step 2.

02. Dust your work surface with icing sugar. Roll out the red sugar paste to a thickness of about 5 mm (¼ in).

03. Using the heart cutter, cut out heart shapes from the red sugar paste. Then pipe on the face details with the black and white royal icing (see page 87). Place the kawaii hearts on top of the cupcakes and serve to your loved ones!

TOP TIP:
You can make the heart shapes in advance, then pop them onto your freshly baked and piped cupcakes.

Teddy Cake Pops

SO CUTE! Cake pops are perfect for parties and presents. You can make these in any colour or play around with different animal shapes. I use my Chocolate Brownie Torte recipe (page 76) here, but you could use any cake pop recipe you like. Fluffy Vanilla Cake (page 72) also works well, with a little buttercream to stick it together. *Makes 12*

 **SKILL LEVEL MODERATE**

01 Break the cake up and pulse a few times in a food processor until you have a sticky crumb. Alternatively, break up the cake with your fingertips until fine and sticky.

02 Take about 30 g (1 oz) of the cake crumb and squeeze together. Roll between your palms to make a ball. You should be able to make 12 balls in total.

03 Melt half the white candy melts in a heatproof bowl over a pan of simmering water. Alternatively, microwave following the packet instructions.

Method continues on the next page...

06 Once the first candy coating on the cake pops has dried, dip the chocolate chips into the melted candy one by one, and press 2 chips against each cake pop to make ears. Return to the fridge for about 15 minutes to set. Pour the excess white candy into a piping bag, to use for the face details.

04 Push a lolly stick into each cake ball. Dip the pops into the melted white candy.

05 Keep the pops upright by sticking into a block of polystyrene or sugar paste, and place in the fridge for 30 minutes.

07 Melt the remaining white candy melts and brown candy melts together to get a nice shade of 'teddy'. Plunge each pop into the chocolate to coat, tapping off any excess. Leave to set in the fridge for 15 minutes.

08 Once set, pipe little white details onto the ears and make a circle to create the snout. Leave to set in the fridge for about 15 minutes. Finish by piping their cute eyes and nose in black, to bring them to life.

09 Decorate by tying a short length of ribbon at the neck of each teddy pop.

Pastel Kawaii  Cake Pops

These are amusing, easy to make – and so kawaii!
They look lovely in all the colours of the rainbow.
As with the Teddy Cake Pops (page 36), you can
also use white chocolate for the first coating, but
any colouring must be oil-based, not water-based.
Makes 12

01 To make the cake pops, follow steps 1–5 for the Teddy Cake Pops on pages 36–38.

02 For the second chocolate coating, dip each pop in a different candy melt colour so you end up with a rainbow of cake pops.

03 Keep the pops upright by sticking into a block of polystyrene or sugar paste. Leave to set in the fridge for 15 minutes.

04 Once the pops are completely dry, add the facial features using black royal icing and pink dusting powder.

STUFF YOU'LL NEED

- about 360 g (12½ oz) ready-baked Chocolate Brownie Torte (page 76)
- 150 g (5 oz) white candy melts
- 12 lolly (popsicle) sticks
- polystyrene block, or pack of sugar paste (fondant), or similar, for drying
- 400 g (14 oz) candy melts, in your choice of colours (I used pink, yellow and mint)
- soft-peak black Royal Icing, (page 89), in a piping bag fitted with number 1.5 round nozzle, for face details
- pink edible dusting powder, for cheeks

SKILL LEVEL
EASY

Mini Christmas Pudding Characters

These little round cakes are made following the same method as the Teddy Cake Pops on page 36, but using a larger quantity of cake – about 90–100 g (3–3½ oz) per pop. Instead of being dipped in candy, they're covered with rolled marzipan or sugar paste (fondant), which keeps the cakes fresher for longer and gives a smoother coating. They work really well using either the Chocolate Brownie Torte (page 76) or the Festive Fruit Cake (page 78). The latter is great for Christmas gifts or fun decorations for the table, as it's easy to mould and lasts for three months. Instead of marzipan, you could use a double coating of sugar paste. *Makes 10*

01 Make balls of cake following steps 1–2 for the Teddy Cake Pops on page 36.

02 Chill for a few hours or freeze for 30 minutes until they are firm enough to work with.

03 Boil some apricot jam with a little added water to thin out, brush over the cake balls and set aside on some baking parchment.

Method continues on the next page...

STUFF YOU'LL NEED

- about 1 kg (2 lb 2 oz) ready-baked Chocolate Brownie Torte (page 76) or Festive Fruit Cake (page 77)
- apricot jam
- 1 kg (2 lb 2 oz) marzipan (optional)
- 1 kg (2 lb 2 oz) brown sugar paste (fondant) (double this if not using marzipan)
- icing (confectioners') sugar, for dusting
- a little brandy, vodka or cooled boiled water
- white sugar paste, for the topping (about 30 g/1 oz per pudding)
- 10 cm (4 in) flower-shaped cutter
- a little white and black soft-peak Royal Icing (page 89), in piping bags fitted with number 2 round nozzles, for sticking and face details
- a little red, green and black sugar paste, for holly, berries and face details
- holly cutter
- small polka dot cutter (optional), for the eyes
- pink edible dusting powder, for cheeks

SKILL LEVEL
MODERATE

04. Roll out a large sheet of marzipan (or sugar paste) to about 5 mm (¼ in) thickness. Cut out squares for covering the cake balls, each measuring about 20 cm (8 in) × 20 cm. This will give enough to cover, with a little excess.

05. Place the covering over the top of each ball and smooth over the sides. Pinch the edges together and cut away the excess. Roll the ball between your palms to smooth. Place the cakes on a cake board dusted with icing sugar to dry for a few hours, or overnight.

06. Brush the balls with brandy, vodka or water. Roll out the brown sugar paste to form a large sheet, then cut into squares as above, making sure the squares are large enough to cover the entire ball. Smooth over the tops and sides, lift up and pinch the edges to seal the coating on the underside of the balls.

07. To make the white 'dripping' icing for your puddings, dust your work surface with icing sugar. Roll out the white sugar paste to a thickness of about 5 mm (¼ in).

Cut out the shapes using the flower-shaped cutter. Keep the excess paste for the eye twinkles.

09 Pipe a small amount of white royal icing onto the top of each cake, press the white 'dripping' over this and smooth down with your fingers.

10 For the final cute details, roll out the red, green and black sugar paste to a thickness of around 5 mm (¼ in) and cut out the holly leaves, berries and eyes. If you don't have a polka dot cutter, simply make a tiny ball for each berry and eye and flatten slightly. Add these to the cakes, sticking them in place with more royal icing.

11 Pipe on the smiles. Finally, place a little white dot of sugar paste over the black eyes to bring out the twinkle, and use pink dusting powder for the cheeks (page 87). So jolly!

08 Flatten the flower shapes slightly using a rolling pin, so that they are about 3 mm (⅛ in) thick.

Christmas Penguin Cake

This little guy is so kawaii with his red bow tie. It's an easy design to do. Follow the instructions on pages 78–79 if you wish to make a layer cake (two layers work well). I love this as it can be on display all holiday and lasts a long time. *Makes 1 cake*

STUFF YOU'LL NEED

- 2 ready-baked 20 cm (8 in) Chocolate Sponge cakes (page 75) or 1 ready-baked 20 cm (8 in) Festive Fruit Cake (page 77)
- icing sugar, for dusting
- 1 kg (2 lb 3 oz) black sugar paste (fondant)
- 100 g (3½ oz) white sugar paste (fondant)
- 50 g (2 oz) orange sugar paste
- a little soft-peak white Royal Icing (page 89), in a piping bag fitted with a number 2 round nozzle, for sticking
- cocktail sticks (optional)
- a little soft-peak red Royal Icing, in a piping bag fitted with a number 2 round nozzle
- edible pink dusting powder, for cheeks

SKILL LEVEL
MODERATE

01 First, fill and crumb coat the cake according to the instructions on pages 78–79, using just 2 layers of cake and 1 kg (2 lb 3 oz) buttercream. Leave to firm up and set in the fridge for 1 hour.

02 To cover the cake, dust your work surface with icing sugar and roll out the black sugar paste to a circle about 5 mm (¼ in) thick, large enough to cover the top and sides. Roll the icing onto the pin, lift up and over the cake and gently smooth it down with your hands. You can place any creases to the back or side of the cake.

03 Once the icing is covering the cake, trim around the base with a sharp knife. Keep the off-cuts to make the wings.

04 Dust your work surface with icing sugar. Roll out the white and orange icing and cut out feet and face shapes using a knife. Stick these to the cake with royal icing. Keep any off-cuts for the eyes and beak.

05 For the little wings, make 2 balls of black sugar paste of equal size, pinch out to a wing shape and attach to the sides of the cake with a little white icing. If you need to, you can use cocktail sticks to prop them up from underneath just while they set. Remove these the following day or when the icing is hard.

06 Roll out a little more black sugar paste and cut two polka dots for eyes (or just flatten two balls) and stick on, piping a little white royal icing over for the sparkle.

07 Using your hands, mould a small beak from the orange sugar paste and stick in place. Pipe on the bow using the red icing. Finally, give him a little blush with some pink dusting powder.

Very Friendly Miniature Ghost Cakes

Who says Halloween has to be terrifying and scary? Make it fun and adorable with these chubby little friendly ghost cakes – the perfect treat for a party or as holiday presents. *Makes 12*

01 Remove the paper cases from the cupcakes. Warm the apricot jam, and brush it over the top and sides of each cupcake. Stick a large marshmallow on top – if they are really big, you can cut these in half.

Method continues on the next page...

STUFF YOU'LL NEED

- 1 batch ready-baked cupcakes (Fluffy Vanilla Cake, page 72)
- apricot jam
- 12 large shop-bought marshmallows (1 per cupcake)
- icing (confectioners') sugar, for dusting
- 1 kg (2 lb 3 oz) white sugar paste (fondant)
- a little soft-peak white Royal Icing (page 89), in a piping bag fitted with a number 2 round nozzle, for sticking
- a little black sugar paste (fondant), for decorating
- 1 cm round cutters, for eyes
- black edible pen (fine-tip), for face details
- pink edible dusting powder, for cheeks

SKILL LEVEL EASY

03 Dust your work surface with icing sugar. Roll out the white sugar paste and cut out squares large enough to cover the top and sides of each cupcake, making sure you have some excess icing.

02 Pop in the microwave for about 10-15 seconds until the marshmallow begins to go squishy and melt onto the cake. Brush a little more jam over the sponge and marshmallow.

04 Place a square of white sugar paste on top of each cupcake and smooth it down with your hands.

05 Cut around the base of the cake, making a little tail to one side. Set aside any off-cuts for making the hands.

07 Finish by rolling out the black sugar paste to 5 mm (¼ in). Cut out circles for the eyes and stick these to the ghosts with a little royal icing. Pipe white dots onto the eyes to add sparkle. Add a cute smile using black edible pen, and dust over some pink powder to make cheeks (page 87).

06 Press the icing gently onto the cake to mould the cute ghostly body. Leave the little tail flowing to one side. To make the ghost hands, use the off-cuts and roll into 24 little balls of icing. Mould these into cones, then flatten slightly and stick 2 to either side of each ghost with white royal icing.

Rainbow &  Clouds Meringue Cake Topper

This is the sweetest rainbow cake topper. It's made with meringue and is so pretty. It's very easy to make – you simply sandwich the two halves together to get it to stand up – but looks so impressive. You can follow the template on page 98, or make any size you wish. Use any strong cake decorating colours, but use gel instead of liquid, or your meringue will be too runny to pipe.
Makes 1 topper

STUFF YOU'LL NEED

- 1 batch Meringue (page 80)
- 1 pre-layered cake, filled and coated (pages 78-79)
- 5 food colouring gels (I used pink, yellow, green, blue and purple)
- 5 small piping bags
- 1 large piping bag fitted with a large round piping nozzle (about 1 cm/½ in)
- rainbow and cloud template (page 98)
- a little stiff-peak white Royal Icing (page 89), for sticking
- cocktail sticks (optional)

**SKILL LEVEL
EASY**

01 Preheat the oven to 120°C (225°F/Gas ½).

02 Split the meringue into 6 small bowls and colour 5 with the food colours.

You can use pastel shades, or add more colour if you want the rainbow to be super-bright.

Method continues on the next page...

03 Trace 2 rainbows on some baking parchment using the template, then turn over. Line a baking tray with the parchment paper.

04 Place each colour of meringue into the small piping bags. Snip the ends off the bags, creating a hole of about 5 mm (¼ in). Place the white meringue for the clouds in the large piping bag, fitted with a large round nozzle.

05 Using the different colours, pipe the rainbow over your template, building up from the bottom to the top.

TOP TIP:
See full size rainbow & cloud template on page 98.

06 Finish with the puffy clouds in white at the bottom of the rainbow.

07 Pop in the oven and bake for about 30 minutes at 120°C (225°F/Gas ½), then reduce the heat to 90°C (175 °F/Gas ¼) for about 20–30 minutes to fully dry out, but not to colour – you need the white to stay as light as possible.

08 To stick together, use a little stiff royal icing and sandwich the 2 halves together. To stand them on the top of your cake, use a touch of royal icing to secure in place. If you wish, you can place 2 cocktail sticks behind the rainbow while it is setting. If you are transporting the cake, pop 2 sticks in front and 2 behind.

Meringue Snowmen

I love these adorable snowmen with their oversized heads – they are so special. They were inspired by some little kawaii keyrings I saw on Pinterest. They're delicious treats and easy to make.
Makes 10

01 Preheat the oven to 120°C (225°F/Gas ½).

02 Trace the snowman shapes on some baking parchment and turn it over. Line 2 baking trays with the parchment.

03 Place the meringue in the piping bag with the large nozzle.

04 Pipe over the templates to fill the body and head, making them nice and chubby.

05 Bake for 30 minutes. Reduce the oven temperature to 90°C (175°F/Gas ¼) and bake for a further 30 minutes until dry, but with a slightly chewy centre. Turn off the oven and leave there until completely cool, about 20-30 minutes, to fully dry out, but not to colour – you need the white to stay as light as possible.

06 To make the scarves, dust your work surface with icing sugar. Roll out the sugar paste fairly thinly. Cut long and short strips of the paste about 1 cm (½ in) wide. You can use a knife to gently cut fringing into the ends of the scarves.

07 Pipe a tiny bit of white royal icing onto the necks of the snowmen, then stick on the scarves.

08 Pipe the face and button details with black and pink royal icing, and draw stripes onto the scarves with the red and blue edible pens. Leave to dry for a few hours. These will keep for up to 1 week if stored in an airtight container or wrapped in a food bag.

STUFF YOU'LL NEED

- 2 batches Meringue (page 80)
- template on page 97
- large piping bag fitted with a large round piping nozzle (about 1 cm/½ in)
- icing (confectioners') sugar, for dusting
- 75g (2½ oz) white sugar paste (fondant)
- soft-peak white Royal Icing (page 89), in a piping bag fitted with a number 2 round nozzle, for sticking
- soft-peak black Royal Icing (page 89), in a piping bag fitted with a number 1.5 round nozzle, for face details
- a little soft-peak pink Royal Icing (page 89), in a piping bag fitted with a number 1.5 round nozzle, for mouth
- red and blue edible food pens (fine-tip), for scarves

SKILL LEVEL EASY

Super-Cute Kawaii Cat Doughnuts

These lovable cat doughnuts are really fun and easy to make and are a delicious treat! The recipe is for a baked doughnut rather than fried — it's easy to pick up doughnut pans in store or online fairly cheaply. If you don't have one you can make them in a cupcake tin — but, of course, there'll be no hole! Alternatively, you can buy some ready-made doughnuts. If you want to add cheeks, you'll need some pink candy melts. *Makes 12*

STUFF YOU'LL NEED

- 1 batch ready-baked doughnuts (page 81) or 12 shop-bought doughnuts
- 600 g (1 lb 5 oz) candy melts in white and any other colours of your choice (I used yellow, pink, green and brown)
- about 30 g (1 oz) white sugar paste (fondant) or marzipan, for ears
- black soft-peak Royal Icing (page 89), in a piping bag fitted with a number 1.5 round nozzle, for face details

SKILL LEVEL EASY

01 Melt the white candy melts according to the packet instructions, or in a heatproof bowl over a pan of simmering water — do not allow the bowl to come into contact with the water.

02 To make the little ears, mould small balls of sugar paste or marzipan to make cones — you'll need 2 per doughnut (see photo on page 81).

03 Dunk the ears in the melted candy and stick them to the top of each doughnut. Chill for 10 minutes in the freezer or 30 minutes in the fridge, keeping the remaining white candy warm.

04 Dunk the doughnuts in the white candy to make the first coating. This will seal the ears in place. Pop onto a wire rack and allow to set for 10 minutes or so.

05 Melt the coloured candy melts. Dip the cats into the colours for a cute two-tone effect. Leave to dry again on the rack.

06 To finish, pipe on the whiskers, eyes and smile using black royal icing. These are best eaten on the day they are made.

TOP TIP: You can add a dab of pink candy to make sweet cheeks.

Choux Babies

I love these cute pastries. Essentially, they're mini éclairs, dipped into candy melts and piped with royal icing. I was inspired to make them when I saw some kawaii plush cushions. I think they look funny and a bit like a cat emoji! They are delicious filled with simple whipped double (heavy) cream with a dash of vanilla extract, or you can use vanilla buttercream (page 86) or crème pâtissière. Don't be daunted by the idea of choux pastry – it is really not difficult and it's fast to make. *Makes 20*

STUFF YOU'LL NEED

- 1 batch Choux Pastry (page 82) in a large piping bag, fitted with a large, fine-toothed round piping nozzle (about 1 cm/½ in)
- 400 g (14 oz) Vanilla Whipped Cream (page 83), in a piping bag fitted with a number 2 round piping nozzle
- 400 g (14 oz) candy melts in pink and grey, or other colours of your choice
- soft-peak black Royal Icing (page 89), in a piping bag fitted with a 1.5 round nozzle, for face details

SKILL LEVEL EASY

01 Preheat the oven to 190°C (375°F/Gas 5). Line a large baking tray, or 2 smaller ones, with baking parchment. Draw chubby éclair shapes about 8 cm (3 in) in length and 2.5 cm (1 in) wide on the parchment, trying to keep them equally sized and leaving a gap of around 2.5 cm (1 in) between each one. Turn the paper over and pipe the choux dough over the shapes.

02 Pop in the oven and bake for around 25 minutes or until puffy, crisp and golden. Immediately pierce little holes on the top of each one with a small, sharp knife to allow the steam to escape. Cool on a rack. Once cool, fill by piercing the base of the buns with the nozzle and piping in the vanilla whipped cream or other filling of choice.

03 Decorate in the same way as the Super-Cute Kawaii Cat Doughnuts (page 58, step 5) by dunking into melted candy melts, drying on a wire rack and piping ears, feet and face decorations using black royal icing.

Bunny & Panda  Bear Macaroons

STUFF YOU'LL NEED

- 1 batch Macaroons (page 84)
- large piping bag fitted with a large round piping nozzle (about 1 cm/½ in)
- small piping bag fitted with a number 3 round piping nozzle
- templates on page 93
- 200 g (7 oz) Basic Vanilla Bean buttercream (page 100), coloured using pale pink food colouring gel
- black and pink edible food pens (fine-tip), for face details

SKILL LEVEL MODERATE

These are to die for – a perfect, delicate teatime treat with a kawaii twist. The bunnies and pandas are lovely in simple white, so they are easy to make. If you like, you can colour the macaroon mix right at the end of the meringue-whisking stage, once the sugar syrup has been added. *Makes 12 macaroons*

01 Preheat the oven to 160°C (320°F/Gas 3).

02 Trace the bunny and panda shapes onto baking parchment and turn it over. Line 2 baking trays with the paper.

03 Place three-quarters of the macaroon mixture into the large piping bag, and the remaining quarter in the small piping bag.

04 Pipe over the templates, using the bag with the large nozzle for the faces and the smaller one for the ears.

05 Bang the trays on the work surface to knock out any air bubbles. Leave the trays out for around 1 hour at room temperature until a skin forms on the surface.

06 Bake the macaroons for 7–8 minutes, then open the oven and wave the door a couple of times to release any steam (be careful not to touch the hot oven!). Close the door and continue cooking for about 7 more minutes. Remove the macaroons and allow to cool completely.

07 Once you are ready to decorate and fill the shapes, pair up the macaroons first, as they will vary in size.

08 Using edible pens in black and pink, draw little faces on one macaroon from each pair (page 87). Colour the panda ears black.

09 To sandwich the shapes together, pipe the pink buttercream around the inside edge of one of each pair of macaroons, then fill in the centre. Gently press the macaroons together so you can see the pale pink filling.

Unicorn Rainbow Chocolate Candy Bark

Rainbow colours and sweets are all swirled together and set in white chocolate – so bright and sweet, it makes a perfect treat. Unicorn bark is super-easy to make and you are sure to delight friends and family. You can break it into shards and pop it into gift boxes or bags, or even use the pieces for cool cake decorations! *Makes 1 large slab*

STUFF YOU'LL NEED

- a little oil, for greasing
- 450 g (1 lb) white chocolate
- 600 g (1 lb 5 oz) candy melts in colours of choice (I used pink, yellow and blue)
- cocktail stick or skewer
- selection of sweets (candy) and sprinkles (I used Smarties® (M&Ms®), hearts, sugar strands and gold and silver balls)

SKILL LEVEL EASY

01 Oil a shallow baking tray measuring approximately 30 × 40 cm (12 × 16 in) and line with a sheet of baking parchment. Lightly oil the parchment too.

02 Melt all the chocolate and candy melts, keeping the colours separate, either in a heatproof bowl over a pan of simmering water (don't let the bowl touch the water), or in a microwave, according to the packet instructions.

03 Pour the white chocolate into the tray and tap it on the work surface to settle. Drizzle over the different candy colours in random lines and swirls – this part is really fun and satisfying!

04 Now take a cocktail stick or skewer and drag it through the colours vertically and then horizontally, to create large marble swirls of colour. Tap the tray gently on the work surface and leave for about 5 minutes so it hardens slightly. Generously scatter sprinkles and sweets all over the bark to decorate. Leave to set in the fridge for about 1 hour.

05 Remove the unicorn bark from the tray and carefully peel off the parchment paper. Smash or cut into large shards using your hands, a rolling pin or a sharp knife.

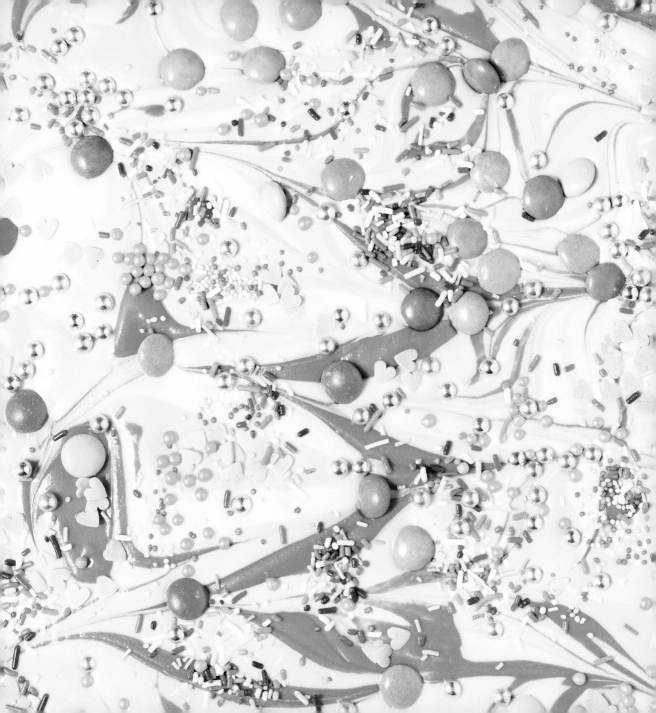

Squishy Marshmallow Cloud Floaties

Make delicious hot chocolate or other drinks even more fantastic by adding floating clouds. They are easy to make and a great idea for special occasions. You can make a large batch and keep them for a few weeks in a plastic container, ready to drop into your drink whenever you fancy a cheery cloud smiling up at you! If you don't have edible pens you can use soft-peak Royal Icing (page 89) and edible dusting powder for the faces. If you use a smaller dish, the clouds will be a little more chunky but will still cut out fine. *Makes about 30 clouds*

STUFF YOU'LL NEED

- 1 batch Marshmallow (page 85)
- oil, for greasing
- icing (confectioners') sugar, for dusting
- cornflour, for dusting
- cloud-shaped cutter
- black and pink edible food pens (fine-tip), for face details

SKILL LEVEL EASY

01 Line a shallow baking tray measuring around 30 × 40 cm (12 × 16 in) with cling film (plastic wrap), then lightly oil. Using a sieve, dust generously with icing sugar and cornflour.

02 Pour the marshmallow mixture into the prepared dish and level out with a damp palette knife. Leave for at least 2 hours to set.

03 Dust the work surface with more sieved icing sugar and cornflour. Carefully lift out the marshmallow and turn it out onto the dusted surface. Flip back over so the upper side with fresh dusting is at the top.

04 Cut into cloud shapes using the cutter and roll them in the sugar and cornflour.

05 Add the faces with black and pink edible pens and leave to dry on a rack for a couple of hours before wrapping or storing.

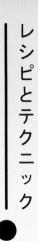

レシピとテクニック

Recipes & Techniques

Vanilla Sugar Cookies

These cookies make adorable home-baked treats for friends and family. This recipe is easy to make and work with. The dough can be cut into any shapes you wish, either with cutters or card templates (see pages 90–98). Simply cut around the template with a sharp knife, cutting wheel or scalpel. If you want to bake these in advance, place them in sealed plastic food bags and stack in flat piles so they don't break. They will keep for up to eight weeks in an airtight container in a cool, dry place. Make sure your ingredients are all at room temperature.

I used this recipe for the Unicorn Poop Iced Gem Cookies (page 9), Lambykins Cookies (page 10), Avocados (page 15), Piñata Cloud Cookies (page 16), Kitty Cookies (page 20) and Best Friends (page 23). *Makes 20–24 medium cookies*

STUFF YOU'LL NEED

- 200 g (7 oz/1¾ sticks) soft salted butter, at room temperature
- 200 g (7 oz/1 cup) golden caster (superfine) sugar
- 2 teaspoons vanilla extract or vanilla bean paste, or 1 vanilla pod
- 1 large free-range egg, lightly beaten
- 400 g (14 oz/3¼ cups) plain (all-purpose) flour, sifted, plus extra for dusting

 SKILL LEVEL EASY

FLAVOUR SWITCH-UPS

 Chocolate:
switch 2 tablespoons flour for 2 tablespoons cocoa powder.

 Lemon or orange:
add the zest of 2 lemons or 1 large orange.

 Spiced cookies:
add a pinch of ginger and 1 teaspoon cinnamon.

01 Preheat the oven to 180°C (350°F/Gas 4) and line a baking tray with parchment paper.

02 Put the butter and sugar into a mixing bowl. Add the vanilla extract or paste, or scrape out the seeds from the vanilla pod and add these. Mix on slow speed in an electric mixer or beat by hand until just combined.

03 Add the egg and mix, still on a slow speed, or use a wooden spoon, until fully incorporated.

04 Tip in all the flour and continue to mix until a dough is formed. If the mixture is a little sticky, add a little more flour. If it's a bit dry, add a few drops of water. You'll know it's the right consistency when the dough comes together without leaving sticky traces on the bowl and forms a nice, shiny, pliable ball.

05 Roll the dough out on a clean, floured surface – use plenty of flour to prevent sticking. If you have them, use guide sticks for rolling out the dough. This will ensure you get an even thickness and the cookies bake evenly. Otherwise, just take care to apply even pressure. Roll to a thickness of about 5 mm (¼ in).

06 Once the dough is rolled out, cut your shapes out with cookie cutters or your chosen card template. Simply trace over the template and stick to a piece of card, then cut around this.

07 Use a palette knife or cake slice to pick up the cookies and transfer them to the lined baking tray. Leave a gap of about 2.5 cm (1 in) between each one.

08 Place in the oven and bake for around 10–12 minutes (for small to medium-sized cookies). Check after 10 minutes, as all ovens vary. The cookies should be golden brown, firm and springy to the touch.

09 Cool on a wire rack and decorate as required.

TOP TIP:
To check if the cookies are done, press the dough with your finger (don't burn yourself!) If your finger leaves an indentation, they're not quite ready so bake a little longer until firm.

Fluffy Vanilla Cake

You can use this recipe to make simple vanilla cupcakes or bake in larger tins for layer cakes. I've used this recipe for the Sweet Unicorn Cake (page 29), Rainbow Swirl Cupcakes (page 32) and Very Friendly Miniature Ghost Cakes (page 48). Make sure your ingredients are all at room temperature. *Makes 12–16 cupcakes, depending on size, or 2 × 20 cm (8 in) round sponge layers*

STUFF YOU'LL NEED

- 300 g (10½ oz/2½ sticks) soft salted butter, at room temperature, plus extra for greasing
- 300 g (10½ oz/1½ cups) golden caster (superfine) sugar
- 2 teaspoons vanilla bean paste or vanilla extract
- 6 medium free-range eggs, lightly beaten
- 300 g (10½ oz/2½ cups) self-raising flour, sifted
- 1 teaspoon baking powder

SKILL LEVEL
EASY

FLAVOUR SWITCH-UPS

 Lemon or orange: add the zest of 2 lemons or 1 large orange.

 Brown sugar/caramel: switch the sugar for light muscovado for a deeper caramel taste.

 Chocolate: switch 2 tablespoons flour for cocoa and add an extra ½ teaspoon baking powder to the dry ingredients.

01 Preheat the oven to 180°C (350 °F/Gas 4). Grease 2 × 20 cm (8 in) round cake tins or a 12-hole cupcake tray.

02 Place the butter, sugar and vanilla or other flavourings into a mixing bowl and combine. If using an electric mixer, turn the speed to high (or if you're using a wooden spoon, use plenty of elbow grease!) and beat until the mixture is very pale, soft and fluffy and the granules of sugar have disappeared.

03 Add the beaten eggs, about one-quarter at a time, beating them in slowly each time.

04 Add the flour gradually, one-quarter at a time, mixing gently on a slow speed, until it has mostly been incorporated. Then, add the baking powder. Fold with a metal spoon if doing this by hand. Take care not to mix or beat vigorously or your sponge can turn out a bit tough. Scrape the mixture into cupcake cases or lined tins as required.

05 For cupcakes, bake for around 12–15 minutes, checking every few minutes. For a larger cake, begin checking after 20 minutes. Remember, all ovens vary so if in doubt use an oven thermometer. The cakes should be a light golden brown, springy to the touch. A sharp knife or metal skewer should come out clean and free of mixture when inserted into the centre.

06 Leave to cool for a couple of minutes in the tins, then turn out onto a cooling rack.

SHELF-LIFE & STORAGE

Cupcakes: once these are iced they will last well for 2–3 days. If frozen, they'll keep for 1 month. I use a corrugated cupcake box with little inserts to keep them in shape, then wrap cling film (plastic wrap) around the box. Allow to come to room temperature for 3–4 hours before using.

Larger cakes: these can be double-wrapped in cling film and popped into a freezer bag with a bag tie for up to 1 month. Remove from the freezer the night before using.

Gingerbread

Gingerbread cookies make perfect gifts for everyone and will keep for up to 12 weeks in an airtight container in a cool, dry place. I used these for the Gingerbread Christmas Decorations on page 27. *Makes 16–20 medium cookies*

01 Mix the golden syrup, orange juice, sugar, spices and vanilla extract in a pan and heat, stirring regularly, over a low to medium heat until all the sugar is dissolved and everything melted and well combined. Do not let the mixture boil. Add the butter and stir gently until melted and incorporated into the hot sugar mix.

02 Add the bicarbonate of soda and whisk until fluffy, puffy and paler in colour.

03 Tip into a mixing bowl and allow to cool slightly. Add all the flour and beat on slow in an electric mixer or mix with a wooden spoon until the mixture comes together and resembles an oily dough. It should be a gloopy, pliable, runny mix, which will harden as it cools and sets.

04 Using a spatula, tip the dough onto 2 large pieces of clingfilm laid out in a cross, one over the other. Wrap up to seal. Chill for at least 2 hours before rolling out, or leave overnight in a fridge.

05 You can freeze the dough at this stage for up to a month. To defrost, place in the fridge overnight, then leave at room temperature for an hour before kneading until pliable.

06 To use, treat in the same way as the Vanilla Sugar Cookies on page 70, but give them a little more room on the tray as they expand during baking. They should also be cooked through and darker. If the dough is too stiff to roll, microwave for 5–10 seconds to soften.

STUFF YOU'LL NEED

- 5 tablespoons golden syrup
- 2 tablespoons orange juice
- 100 g (3½ oz/½ cup) molasses sugar or dark brown sugar
- 1 tablespoon ground ginger
- ½ tablespoon ground cinnamon
- 1 teaspoon vanilla extract or vanilla bean paste
- 100 g (3½ oz/⅞ stick) butter, diced
- 1 scant teaspoon bicarbonate of soda (baking soda)
- 240 g (8½ oz/2 cups) plain (all-purpose) flour

SKILL LEVEL EASY

Chocolate Sponge

I love this recipe – it's rich and soft, unlike some chocolate sponge recipes that can be very dry. You can use this for the layer cake designs, such as the Sweet Unicorn Cake (page 29) or the Christmas Penguin Cake (page 46). Make sure the ingredients are at room temperature. *Makes 12–16 cupcakes, depending on size, or 2 × 20 cm (8 in) round sponge layers*

01 Preheat the oven to 180°C (350°F/Gas 4).

02 Place the chocolate, sugar and butter in a heatproof bowl. Put in the microwave on medium power for 1 minute intervals, stirring at each interval, until melted. Alternatively, place the bowl over a pan of simmering water. Do not allow the bowl to touch the water. Allow to cool slightly.

03 Whisk the eggs, sour cream and vanilla extract together. Mix together the flour and cocoa powder.

04 Add the egg mixture to the melted chocolate mix and stir well.

05 Fold in the flour and cocoa. Spoon into cupcake cases to just over half full, or into 2 × 20 cm (8 in) round tins, greased and lined with baking parchment.

06 If making cupcakes, bake for 15-20 minutes until just firm. If making layer cakes, bake for 20-25 minutes. A knife or skewer inserted into the centre should come out slightly sticky (but not wet) when it's cooked – not clean, as you'd expect from a vanilla sponge. Leave cupcakes to cool in the tray. For layer cakes, leave to cool for a couple of minutes before turning out onto a wire rack.

Chocolate Brownie Torte

This is a lovely, rich recipe, and would be a good alternative for a kawaii Christmas cake for those who don't like fruit cake. It's the best recipe I know for making cake pops. You can use an electric mixer with a paddle or beater attachment, a hand-held mixer, or the old-fashioned method – a wooden spoon, whisk, extra time and elbow grease! The cake will keep nicely for up to two weeks. *Makes 2 × 20 cm (8 in) round cakes*

STUFF YOU'LL NEED

- 225 g (8 oz/1⅓ cups) plain chocolate chips (70 per cent cocoa solids)
- 250 g (9 oz/2¼ sticks) soft unsalted butter
- 350 g (12 oz/1¾ cups) light muscovado sugar
- 6 medium free-range eggs, beaten with 2 teaspoons vanilla extract
- 225 g (8 oz/1¾ cups) plain (all-purpose) flour
- Belgian Chocolate Ganache Buttercream (page 87) (optional)

 SKILL LEVEL EASY

01 Preheat the oven to 140°C (275°F/Gas 1). Grease and line 2 × 20 cm (8 in) cake tins.

02 Place the chocolate in a microwave-safe bowl and heat on medium power in the microwave for 1 minute at a time, until just melted, stirring at each interval. Alternatively, place in a heatproof bowl over a pan of just simmering water. Do not let the bowl touch the water. Allow to cool.

03 Beat the butter and sugar slowly until combined, then turn up the speed to maximum and continue to beat until pale and fluffy.

04 Add the beaten eggs and vanilla a little at a time, beating slowly, until each batch is incorporated.

05 Pour all the cooled chocolate into the mix, beating continuously.

06 Fold in the flour until just incorporated. Spoon evenly into the tins and bake for 25–35 minutes. Check every 5 minutes as all ovens vary.

07 The cakes should be well risen, but still wobble a bit when shaken. The crust will sink back into the cakes as they cool. Leave to cool in the tin.

08 If making a layer cake, sandwich the cakes together with a filling of Belgian chocolate ganache buttercream.

Festive Fruit Cake

STUFF YOU'LL NEED

- 275 g (10 oz/1¾ cups) raisins
- 275 g (10 oz/1¾ cups) currants
- 175 g (6 oz/1 cup) sultanas
- 75 g (2½ oz/½ cup) mixed peel
- 225 g (8 oz/2⅜ cups) natural-colour glacé cherries, washed and halved
- 150 g (5 oz/1¼ sticks) salted butter
- 150 g (5 oz/¾ cup) molasses sugar
- 3 medium eggs, beaten with 1 tablespoon vanilla extract
- ½ teaspoon ground cinnamon
- ½ teaspoon ground ginger
- ¼ teaspoon ground nutmeg
- pinch of ground cloves
- ½ teaspoon mixed spice
- 140 g (4½ oz/1⅛ cups) plain (all-purpose) flour
- 120 ml (4 fl oz/½ cup) brandy, plus more to feed (about 6-10 tablespoons, to taste)
- 50 ml (2 fl oz/¼ cup) vodka

SKILL LEVEL EASY

This is the best recipe ever! It's delicious, and perfect for the holidays. It doesn't need long to improve in flavour once baked – a couple of weeks is fine. You could also make it a few months in advance and keep it wrapped, feeding it occasionally with more brandy. I have used this for the Mini Christmas Pudding Characters (page 42) and Christmas Penguin Cake (page 46). *Makes 1 × 20 cm (8 in) cake*

01 Preheat the oven to 140°C (275°F/Gas 1). Grease and line a deep 20 cm (8 in) cake tin.

02 Place all the dried fruit, peel and glacé cherries into a large bowl big enough to hold the entire mixture and stir to combine with a large wooden spoon or your hands.

03 Place the butter and sugar in a small, microwave-safe bowl and heat for 1 minute intervals on medium power, stirring with a whisk at each interval, to mix the butter and sugar together. If you don't have a microwave, do this in a non-stick pan over a low heat.

04 Add the spices to the flour and mix well with a metal spoon to disperse.

05 Tip the warm butter and sugar mixture into the large bowl of fruit and stir well. Add the beaten eggs and vanilla and mix well. Add the flour and spice mix and stir in until just mixed. Finally, add the brandy and vodka. Pour the mixture into the tin.

06 Place the tin in the oven and bake for 1 hour, then turn the heat down to 125°C (250°F/Gas ½) and continue to bake until completely cooked through. This will take approximately 2–2½ hours, depending on your oven. Check that a sharp knife or a skewer comes out almost clean.

Layering & Crumb Coating a Cake

Creating cake layers is such an easy process, once you know how. I've used this technique for the Sweet Unicorn Cake (page 29) and the Christmas Penguin Cake (page 46).

Recipes & Techniques

STUFF YOU'LL NEED

- 4 ready-baked 20 cm (8 in) round Fluffy Vanilla Cakes (page 72), coloured with pastel food colouring gels, if desired
- turntable (optional)
- 2 kg (4 lb 6 oz) Basic Vanilla Bean Buttercream (page 86)
- 20 cm (8 in) cake drum and 30 cm (12 in) cake drum, for display
- large palette knife
- apricot jam (optional)

SKILL LEVEL
MODERATE

01 If you have a turntable, this will make it easier, but you can also just use your work surface. Using a little buttercream, stick the bottom cake layer onto the smaller cake drum and make it sure it is centred.

02 Spread a layer of buttercream over the first cake layer, then place the second cake layer on top. Repeat this process with the next 2 layers.

03 Using a palette knife, generously spread buttercream all around the sides of the cake. You can press on the top of the cake to hold it still. Fill in any gaps and smooth over.

06 You can now place the cake in the fridge for 1 hour to set. If you do this, brush over some warmed apricot jam so that any sugar paste you apply later sticks to the cake.

04 Once the sides are covered, spread a layer of buttercream over the top. Using the palette knife, sweep all around the cake with a firm pressure. Keep the knife or scraper straight, to smooth off the excess and make the surface as flat as you can.

05 With a back-and-forth motion, smooth over the top to neaten. Go around the edge again if you need to. Remove any lumpy areas around the top edge with a small, sharp knife.

Meringue

You'll need one quantity of this for the Rainbow & Clouds Meringue Cake Topper (page 52) and two quantities to make the Meringue Snowmen (page 56).

01 Preheat the oven to 120°C (225°F/Gas ½) and line a baking tray with parchment paper. If you're using a template, trace any shapes onto the paper first and turn it over.

02 Place the sugars in a bowl and stir with a spoon or whisk to combine.

03 Whisk the egg whites and salt in a completely clean and grease-free bowl until you reach stiff-peak consistency.

04 Add one-third of the sugar and mix thoroughly with an electric whisk on a fast speed for about 30 seconds. Repeat with two further additions of the sugar until you have a stiff and glossy mixture. Use as required in the recipe.

STUFF YOU'LL NEED

- 75 g (2½ oz/⅔ cups) icing (confectioners') sugar
- 75 g (2½ oz/⅓ cup) white caster (superfine) sugar
- 3 medium free-range egg whites (at room temperature)
- pinch of salt

 SKILL LEVEL EASY

STUFF YOU'LL NEED

- 12-hole doughnut pan
- 200 g (7 oz/1¾ cups) plain (all-purpose) flour
- 175 g (6 oz/⅞ cup) golden caster (superfine) sugar
- 2 teaspoons baking powder
- ½ teaspoon ground cinnamon
- 250 ml (8 fl oz/1 cup) buttermilk
- 2 medium free-range eggs, lightly beaten
- 30 g (1 oz/¼ stick) butter, melted, plus extra for greasing
- 1 teaspoon vanilla extract
- large piping bag

SKILL LEVEL EASY

Doughnuts

Use this recipe for the Super-Cute Kawaii Cat Doughnuts (page 58). *Makes 12 large doughnuts*

01 Preheat the oven to 220°C (430°F/Gas 9). Lightly grease a 12-hole doughnut pan.

Place all the dry ingredients together in a bowl and mix well with a whisk to distribute the spices and mix thoroughly.

02 Add the wet ingredients and mix until combined. Try not to overmix.

03 Pour the batter into a piping bag and fill the doughnut pan until it's approximately three-quarters full. Do this in batches if necessary.

04 Bake for 7–9 minutes until baked through and the tops are springy to the touch. Allow to cool for a couple of minutes, then turn out onto a wire rack to cool completely. Decorate as required.

Choux Pastry

You can use this recipe for the Choux Babies on page 60. *Makes 20*

01 Preheat the oven to 190°C (375°F/Gas 5). Bring the water, milk, butter, sugar and salt to the boil in a saucepan.

02 Once boiling remove from the heat, throw in all the flour at once and beat well with a wooden spoon.

03 Return to a gentle heat and cook, stirring continuously, for 1 minute.

04 Place in an electric mixer or a bowl, and allow to cool slightly. Beat in the eggs, one at a time, until completely combined. You can do this by hand with a spoon if you don't have a mixer – it will just take a bit longer.

05 Once ready, transfer the mixture to the piping bag and leave to sit for 10 minutes, before piping as required.

STUFF YOU'LL NEED

- 60 ml (2 fl oz/¼ cup) water
- 60 ml (2 fl oz/¼ cup) full-fat (whole) milk
- 60 g (2 oz/½ stick) unsalted butter
- 2 teaspoons golden caster (superfine) sugar
- pinch of salt
- 100 g (3½ oz/⅞ cups) bread flour
- 4 medium free-range eggs

SKILL LEVEL EASY

Vanilla Whipped Cream

This is a really quick and easy recipe to use either as a topping or a filling inside cakes like the little Choux Babies on page 60. *Makes 300 g (10 oz)*

01 Using a whisk, whip the cream with the sugar until thickened and just holding soft peaks.

02 Add the vanilla paste and whip a little more. Be careful not to overwhip the cream as it will thicken slightly when you take it out of the bowl.

03 Place in a piping bag and use as required in the recipe.

TOP TIP:
To fill pastries, it is easier to pipe with a long round nozzle to help push the cream into the buns. However, if you don't have a nozzle, you can cut a small hole (about 0.5 cm/¼ in) in the piping bag and pierce each pastry with a knife. Push the bag inside, then squeeze the yummy vanilla cream into the pastries.

Macaroons

Use this recipe for the Bunny & Panda Bear Macaroons on page 63. *Makes about 12 macaroon sandwiches*

01 Trace the desired shapes for the macaroons onto baking parchment. Leave a gap of around 2.5 cm (1 in) between each one. Turn the paper over and use to line 2 baking trays.

02 Place the ground almonds and icing sugar in a food processor and pulse several times until really fine. Sieve and discard any large pieces left behind.

03 Place this fine powder in a bowl and add half of the egg whites and the vanilla extract, mixing to make a thick paste.

04 Place the remaining egg whites with a pinch of salt in a completely clean and grease-free bowl. A stand mixer is easiest for this. You can also use an electric hand whisk, but you'll need to keep a close eye on the sugar syrup.

05 Place the sugar and water into a small saucepan and bring to the boil. Once the sugar starts to bubble and the temperature is around 100°C (210°F) when measured with a sugar thermometer, start to whisk the egg whites to a stiff-peak consistency.

06 Once the sugar syrup reaches 115°C (240°F), turn the mixer to maximum speed. Carefully pour the sugar syrup into the eggs in a fine stream towards one side of the bowl (avoiding the whisk), until it is all incorporated. The egg whites will thicken and turn glossy. Continue whisking at maximum speed for about 5–10 minutes until the meringue mix has cooled.

07 Add one-quarter of the meringue mix to the almond paste to loosen, then use a spatula to fold in the remainder until well combined. Do this gently, as you need to keep the air in. When the spatula is lifted, the trail should settle back into the mixture after about 15 seconds. Pour into piping bags and use as required in the recipe.

STUFF YOU'LL NEED

- 160 g (5½ oz/1⅔ cups) ground almonds (almond meal)
- 160 g (5½ oz/1¾ cups) icing (confectioners') sugar
- 120 ml (4 fl oz/½ cup) egg whites
- 1 teaspoon vanilla extract
- pinch of salt
- 150 g (5 oz/1½ cups) caster (superfine) sugar
- 60 ml (2 fl oz/¼ cup) water
- sugar thermometer

SKILL LEVEL MODERATE

Marshmallow

Use this recipe for the Squishy Marshmallow Cloud Floaties on page 66. *Makes 1 large sheet*

Use this recipe for the Squishy Marshmallow Cloud Floaties on page 66.

STUFF YOU'LL NEED

- **10 sheets leaf gelatine**
- **250 ml (8 fl oz/1 cup) water**
- **sugar thermometer**
- **450 g (1 lb/2½ cups) caster (superfine) sugar**
- **2 egg whites**
- **2 teaspoons vanilla extract**

**SKILL LEVEL
EASY**

01 Soak the gelatine in 160 ml (5½ fl oz/⅔ cup) of the cold water.

02 Put the remaining water in a heavy-based pan with the caster sugar. Bring to the boil and continue cooking for 12–15 minutes until the temperature reaches 115°C (240°F) on a sugar thermometer.

03 Carefully add the gelatine and water to the syrup and mix with a spoon. Pour the syrup into a metal bowl or jug.

04 Place the egg whites into a completely clean and grease-free bowl and beat with an electric whisk until stiff peaks are formed. Pour in the syrup and vanilla extract, whisking continuously. The mixture will start to thicken.

05 Continue whisking for 5–10 minutes until the mixture is stiff enough to hold its shape on the whisk, and the bowl has cooled down and is just warm to the touch. Use as required.

Basic Vanilla Bean Buttercream

A very easy recipe for filling or topping cupcakes and large cakes. I use this for the Sweet Unicorn Cake (page 29) and cupcakes (pages 32 and 35). Make sure to use very soft butter – sometimes I blast mine in the microwave for about 10 seconds. Save the vanilla pod (if using) for flavouring syrups or pop into your sugar jar to infuse the sugar. Like most of the cakes and fillings, you can freeze any you have left over. *Makes 750 g (1 lb 10 oz) (enough to fill and cover a 20 cm (8 in) round cake)*

STUFF YOU'LL NEED

- 1 vanilla pod, or 2 teaspoons vanilla bean paste
- 250 g (9 oz/2¼ sticks) soft unsalted butter
- 2 teaspoons vanilla extract
- 500 g (1 lb 2 oz/4 cups) icing (confectioners') sugar, sieved

SKILL LEVEL EASY

01 If you have an electric stand mixer then use this with the beater or paddle attachment. Otherwise, use a hand-held mixer or a wooden spoon. Scrape the seeds from the vanilla pod, if using, or add the paste. In the mixer or bowl, cream the butter with the vanilla seeds and extract until very pale, creamy and smooth.

02 Add about one-quarter of the icing sugar. To make sure the sugar doesn't puff out in clouds and cover your kitchen, mix slowly at first.

You can also place a damp tea towel over the bowl. Once the icing sugar is incorporated, beat at a high speed for about 1 minute until the mix is really creamy and pale. It will take you a few more minutes by hand.

03 Continue adding the sugar, one quarter at a time, taking care to beat it in well after each addition.

04 Beat the buttercream at high speed for 1–2 minutes until fluffy and pale. Use as required.

FLAVOUR SWITCH-UPS

 Orange Buttercream:
follow the basic recipe above, omitting the vanilla if you prefer. When creaming the butter, add the zest of 2 fresh oranges.

 Raspberry & Strawberry Buttercream:
add 1 tablespoon each of good-quality raspberry and strawberry jam.

 Lemon Buttercream:
add the zest of 1 lemon and a100 g (3½ oz) homemade or good-quality shop-bought lemon curd.

 Belgian Chocolate Ganache Buttercream:
this is perfect as a frosting for the Kawaii Sweetheart Cupcakes (page 35) and to fill and ice the Chocolate Brownie Torte (page 76). Put 75 ml (2½ fl oz/¼ cup) fresh double (heavy) organic cream and 150 g (5 oz) good-quality Belgian chocolate (70 per cent cocoa solids) into a microwave-safe bowl. Heat on medium power for 1 minute at a time, stirring periodically, until you have a smooth velvety ganache. Alternatively, you can do this in a heatproof glass bowl over a pan of gently simmering water. Don't let the bowl touch the water. Leave to cool completely. Once cooled (but still liquid), stir the ganache gently into the buttercream. Make sure it's not warm or it will make your buttercream oily and split!

ADDING KAWAII FACES

There are lots of fun ways to add cute faces to your cakes, biscuits and treats. Soft-peak Royal Icing (pages 88–89) is a brilliant medium as it's easy to use, and can simply be piped on using a number 2 nozzle, or a number 1.5 nozzle for fine details. You can colour it any shade you wish. Candy melts and melted chocolate can also be piped on in the same way.

Kawaii faces can also be drawn onto cakes and biscuits with edible food pens, but note that these don't work well on oil-based cakes or chocolatey surfaces as the ink is repelled from the surface. In this case, it's best to use royal icing.

Edible lustre dusts can be used to add little red cheeks to your faces. Lustre dusts can also be transformed into paints by adding a little liquid such as vodka, gin or even vanilla extract.

If you're using a method you haven't tried before, it's a good idea to practise on a work surface or baking tray before drawing the designs onto your bakes. Kawaii faces should be fun – so enjoy playing around and experimenting!

Royal Icing

As a general rule, I calculate quantities based on 1 egg white for every 250 g (9 oz/2 cups) icing (confectioners') sugar, plus the juice of half a lemon. It's not a precise science. This icing will keep for up to 1 week in a plastic food bag or wrapped pot. When you come to using it, cover it with a clean, damp cloth as you prepare your other ingredients, as it dries out very quickly once exposed to the air. You can also buy ready-made powdered royal icing sugar, to which you just add water.

STUFF YOU'LL NEED

- 250 g (9 oz/2 cups) icing (confectioners') sugar, plus extra if needed
- 1 egg white
- juice of ½ lemon (about 2 tablespoons), plus extra if needed

 SKILL LEVEL EASY

01 Put all the ingredients into a bowl and mix together. If you have a stand mixer, use the paddle attachment and mix on a slow speed. You need to be able to see inside the bowl to check that all the icing sugar has been incorporated, but the mix is still very stiff.

02 If you need a little more liquid, add a dash more lemon juice. If you need a little more sugar to dry the mix, add a handful or so of icing sugar. You want to achieve a thick, stiff paste that isn't powdery dry and really holds its shape.

03 Beat on a slow speed for about 3 minutes to make a smooth icing.

04 Royal icing is one of the handiest mediums for decorating colourful cute cookies with any type of kawaii design you can imagine. It's great for decorating your bakes and cakes too, and is easy to draw with. It's easy to make, and you can also buy royal icing powder in the supermarket – you just need to add water. The most important thing is to get the consistency right, as this will make decorating much easier.

TOP TIP:
If you roll the lemon firmly along the work surface first, it will yield more juice.

STIFF-PEAK

When you make your original batch of royal icing, it should be firm enough so that when you lift a spoon up from the mixture you get a stiff 'peak'. It should look spiky and rigid – almost dry. This means that whatever design you pipe will hold its shape. It can be used to stick decorations onto cakes, secure cakes to their iced drums or hold cake tiers together. It sets very hard, so can hold the weight of a large decoration, for example a large cookie.

When colouring royal icing, use paste or gel food colourings rather than liquid ones. These will not change the consistency of your icing too much. Bear in mind that if you are adding a lot of colour it will make the icing wetter.

SOFT-PEAK

This is when the icing is 'let down' with a few drops of water, lemon juice or egg white if you prefer (use pasteurised), so that it can flow freely from your icing bag.

Use this for piping patterns and kawaii faces or for outlining shapes of cookies. It's not completely runny and the line should still hold its shape. It can also be used for sticking decorations to cakes.

To test, just add a few drops of water at a time until the icing feels easier to stir and is looser. Don't make it too runny! It should still hold a peak, but the peak should glisten and flop over slightly.

RUNNY ICING

This consistency is used for filling in the outlines of cookies or cake decorations. It's important to get it just right.

To test whether the consistency is right, take a palette knife or spoon and drag it through the bowl of icing to a depth of around 3–5 cm (1¼–2 in). Lift the spoon or knife from the bowl to create a trail and count to 10. The trail should disappear after 5–10 seconds. It should be loose enough to flatten out and sit cleanly, without being too runny.

If it takes longer for the trail to disappear, then the icing is too thick, so slowly add a few more drops of water. If the icing surface smooths over in less than 5–10 seconds, it is too runny. Slowly add more sifted icing sugar or a little more stiff-peak royal icing to thicken it. You don't want the icing to be too thick so that it doesn't flood properly, or too thin so that it's very runny and hard to control.

TOP TIP:
Rather than adding water directly, I recommend running a spoon under a tap with a little icing on, then stir this into the icing. It only needs a small amount of liquid to loosen the consistency.

TOP TIP:
Colour runny icing at the stiff-peak stage, before letting it down. This way you won't thin out your perfect runny consistency.

Templates

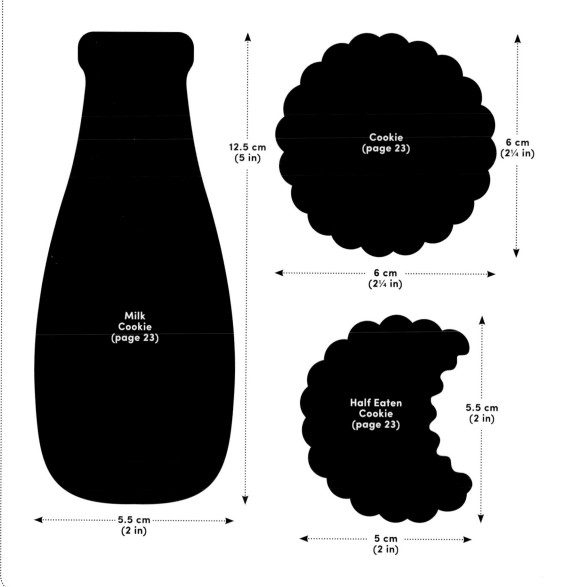

Milk
Cookie
(page 23)

12.5 cm
(5 in)

5.5 cm
(2 in)

Cookie
(page 23)

6 cm
(2¼ in)

6 cm
(2¼ in)

Half Eaten
Cookie
(page 23)

5.5 cm
(2 in)

5 cm
(2 in)

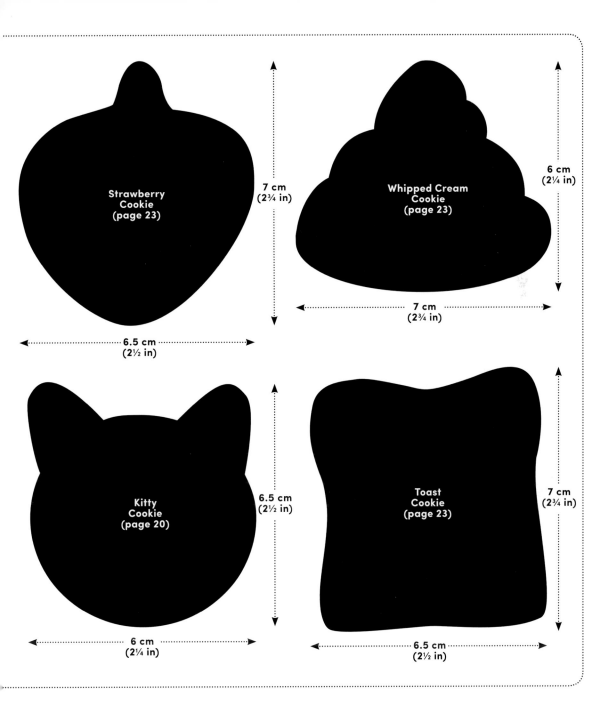

Strawberry Cookie (page 23)

7 cm (2¾ in)

6.5 cm (2½ in)

Whipped Cream Cookie (page 23)

6 cm (2¼ in)

7 cm (2¾ in)

Kitty Cookie (page 20)

6.5 cm (2½ in)

6 cm (2¼ in)

Toast Cookie (page 23)

7 cm (2¾ in)

6.5 cm (2½ in)

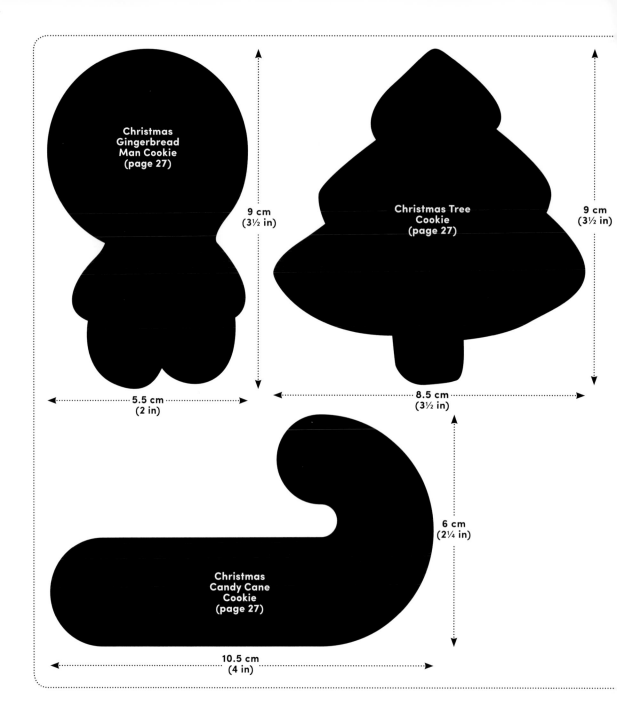

Templates

Christmas Gingerbread Man Cookie (page 27)

9 cm (3½ in)

5.5 cm (2 in)

Christmas Tree Cookie (page 27)

9 cm (3½ in)

8.5 cm (3½ in)

Christmas Candy Cane Cookie (page 27)

6 cm (2¼ in)

10.5 cm (4 in)

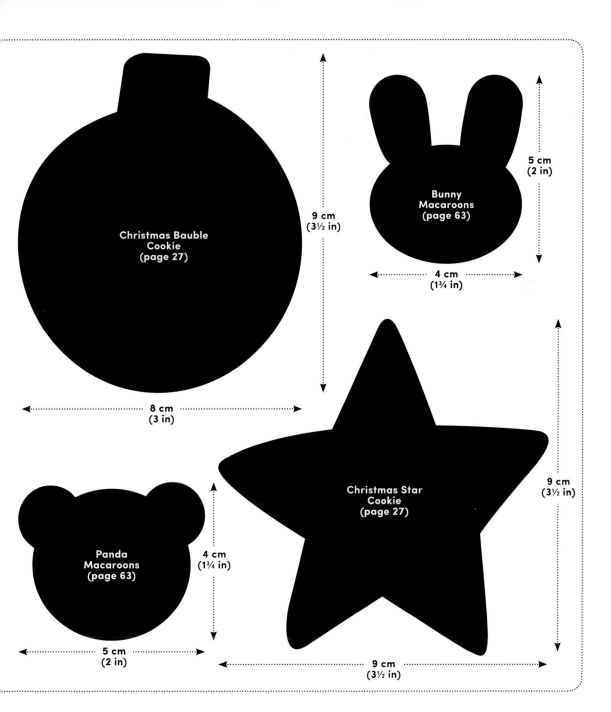

Christmas Bauble
Cookie
(page 27)

9 cm
(3½ in)

8 cm
(3 in)

Bunny
Macaroons
(page 63)

5 cm
(2 in)

4 cm
(1¾ in)

Panda
Macaroons
(page 63)

4 cm
(1¾ in)

5 cm
(2 in)

Christmas Star
Cookie
(page 27)

9 cm
(3½ in)

9 cm
(3½ in)

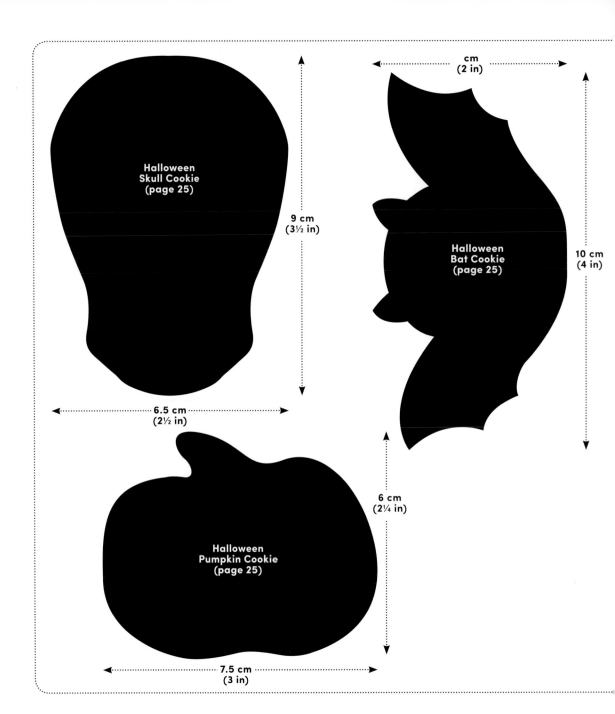

**Halloween
Skull Cookie
(page 25)**

**Halloween
Bat Cookie
(page 25)**

**Halloween
Pumpkin Cookie
(page 25)**

**9 cm
(3½ in)**

**6.5 cm
(2½ in)**

**cm
(2 in)**

**10 cm
(4 in)**

**6 cm
(2¼ in)**

**7.5 cm
(3 in)**

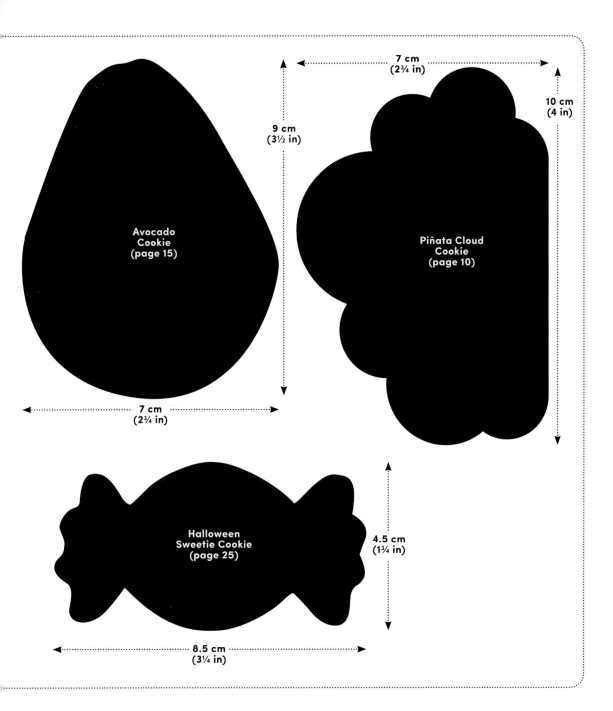

Avocado
Cookie
(page 15)

9 cm
(3½ in)

7 cm
(2¾ in)

7 cm
(2¾ in)

10 cm
(4 in)

Piñata Cloud
Cookie
(page 10)

Halloween
Sweetie Cookie
(page 25)

4.5 cm
(1¾ in)

8.5 cm
(3¼ in)

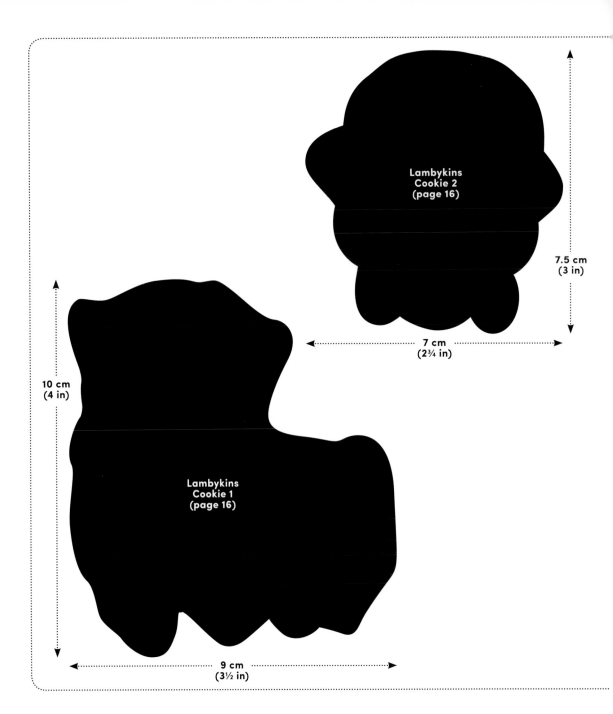

**Lambykins
Cookie 2
(page 16)**

7.5 cm
(3 in)

7 cm
(2¾ in)

10 cm
(4 in)

**Lambykins
Cookie 1
(page 16)**

9 cm
(3½ in)

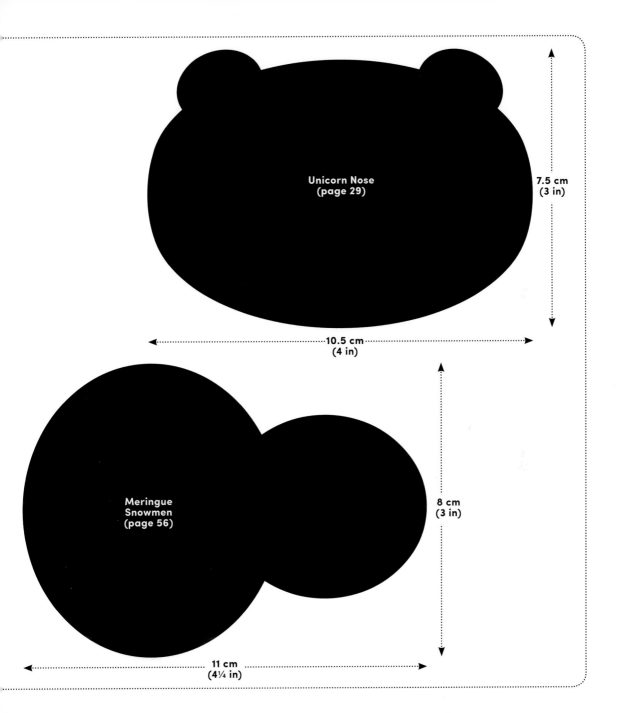

Unicorn Nose
(page 29)

7.5 cm
(3 in)

10.5 cm
(4 in)

Meringue
Snowmen
(page 56)

8 cm
(3 in)

11 cm
(4¼ in)

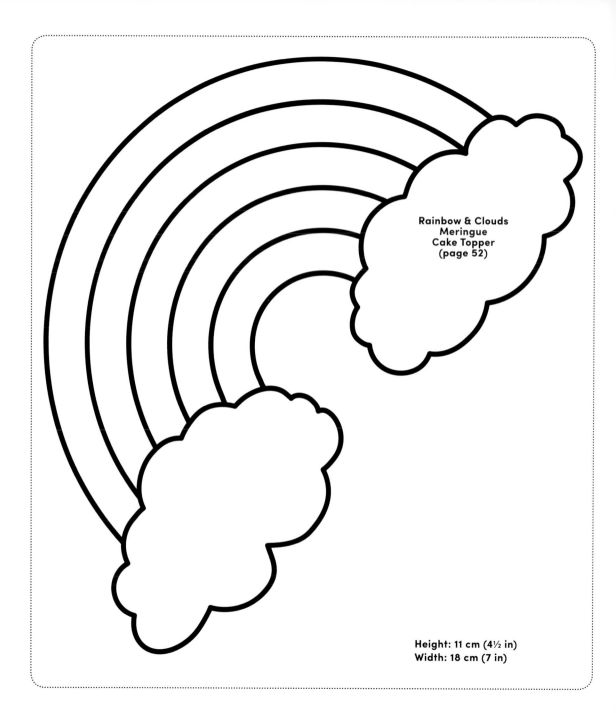

Rainbow & Clouds
Meringue
Cake Topper
(page 52)

Height: 11 cm (4½ in)
Width: 18 cm (7 in)

About The Author

Juliet Sear is a baking expert, food artist, stylist, TV personality and best-selling author. Juliet has over 15 years' experience working in the baking industry and works with global brands developing recipes, online content and experiential edible art installations for PR stunts.

Index

Thank Yous

Thank you for buying Kawaii Cakes! I hope you enjoy all the cuteness as much as I have! You are adorable :)

Thanks to all at Hardie Grant for your help and support. Big love to Jacqui Melville – your pics are amazing and you made the bakes look even more adorable than in real life! Huge thanks to design extraordinaire Claire Warner for this most adorable, colourful, incredible design and illustrations. I love it!

Massive family love to Simon for always being there. You are the peanut butter to my jelly, the milk to my cookie, the cream to my strawberries! To our kids: Lydia, who had fun with me and helped out by adding loads of cute kawaii faces to the bakes we shot, and for coming up with lots of ideas; your artistic skills were invaluable! And to George and Ruby, thanks for being crazy and funny (with a little help from Bhurman), helping me out and being enthusiastic about this book and all my work in the world of food.

As always, huge thanks to nanny Lydia, the best super mother-in-law and friend. To my dad George, kindest man and clever dad and grandad; to my sis Nancy, the best sister ever!

Shout out to clever old bean Juliet Baptiste-Kelly for all your help with *Kawaii Cakes* and more. Team Twoliet all the way!

Lastly, big love to some work allies and good friends with whom I am lucky enough to work and get creative on the food frontier: Katie Masters, Leynah Bruce, my Billington's babes, Matt Nielsen and also the gang at Silverspoon (bakingmad.com). Lovely Ana Thorsdottir and the brilliant Citizen crew. Linda Jones and the Meyer team. Riccardo Panichi and team at Dr O.

Thanks to Natalie Bloxham for believing in me and of course Julia Alger, #teamwork, what fun! To Emma Hart, a beautiful person inside and out and your team at PushPR. To Jen Christie, my lovely literary agent, thanks for always there bigging me up, supporting me and helping writing AND EATING my recipes. Hugs to Kirsty Williams you lovely being, my great friend and agent at Insanity :) Rosana McPhee, Jessy Prestidge, Louise Sansom and Dan O'Malley.

Thanks to KitchenAid, Wilton, Rainbow Dust, SugarShack, Billington's, Nielsen Massey, Dr Oetker and Tatty Devine for your kind contributions to making this book :)

Suppliers

Cake Boss (cakeboss.co.uk)
For bakeware, accessories and more.

Dr Oetker (oetker.co.uk)
For icing, food colouring and more.

Rainbow Dust (rainbowdust.co.uk)
For amazing edible pens, paints, candy and more.

Scrumptious Sprinkles (scrumptious.uk.net)
For the most delicious sprinkles imaginable.

SugarShack (sugarshack.co.uk)
For baking supplies, ingredients, sugarcraft
supplies and more.

Tatty Devine (tattydevine.com)
For amazing rainbow necklaces and more.

Wilton (wilton.com)
For baking and cake supplies including edible
pens, colours, sprinkles, candy melts and more.

Kawaii Cakes by Juliet Sear

First published in 2017 by Hardie Grant Books

Hardie Grant Books (UK)
52–54 Southwark Street
London SE1 1UN
hardiegrant.co.uk

Hardie Grant Books (Australia)
Ground Floor, Building 1
658 Church Street
Melbourne, VIC 3121
hardiegrant.com.au

British Library Cataloguing-in-Publication Data. A catalogue
record for this book is available from the British Library.

ISBN: 978-1-78488-121-4

Publisher: Kate Pollard
Senior Editor: Kajal Mistry
Editorial Assistant: Hannah Roberts
Publishing Assistant: Eila Purvis
Design: Claire Warner Studio
Photography: Jacqui Melville
Prop Stylist: Ginger Whisk
Home Economist: Juliet Baptiste-Kelly
Copy editor: Charlotte Coleman-Smith
Proofreader: Lorraine Jerram
Indexer: Richard Rosenfeld
Colour Reproduction by p2d
Printed and bound in China by 1010

10 9 8 7 6 5 4 3 2 1